From Tadpole to Frog

Following the Life Cycle

by Suzanne Slade

illustrated by Jeff Yesh

PICTURE WINDOW BOOKS

Thanks to our advisers for their expertise:

Don C. Forester, Ph.D., Professor of Biology
Towson University, Maryland

Terry Flaherty, Ph.D., Professor of English
Minnesota State University, Mankato

Editor: Shelly Lyons
Designers: Nathan Gassman and Lori Bye
Page Production: Michelle Biedscheid
Art Director: Nathan Gassman
Associate Managing Editor: Christianne Jones
The illustrations in this book were created digitally.

Photo Credits: © Gustav Verderber/Visuals Unlimited, 23.

Picture Window Books
151 Good Counsel Drive
P.O. Box 669
Mankato, MN 56002-0669
877-845-8392
www.picturewindowbooks.com

Printed in the United States of America.

 All books published by Picture Window Books
are manufactured with paper containing at least
10 percent post-consumer waste.

Library of Congress Cataloging-in-Publication Data
Slade, Suzanne.
From tadpole to frog : following the life cycle / by Suzanne Slade ;
illustrated by Jeff Yesh.
p. cm. — (Amazing science. Life cycle)
ISBN 978-1-4048-4922-8 (library binding)
1. Frogs—Life cycles—Juvenile literature. I. Yesh, Jeff, 1971- ill. II. Title.
QL668.E2S56 2009
597.8'9—dc22   2008006432

Table of Contents

Long-Legged Leapers

Frogs are amazing animals that come in many sizes and colors. These mighty jumpers have long legs for leaping. They also have webbed or partially webbed feet for swimming. With a quick flick of the tongue, a frog can catch a tasty bug. More than 5,500 different kinds of frogs live in wet places around the world. All of them have the same life cycle. This book follows the life cycle of a wood frog.

Frogs are amphibians. They are cold-blooded, have backbones, and can live in water or on land.

From Water to Land

A frog's life begins as a tadpole in the water. Later, the tadpole's body changes so it can live on land. Although frogs can jump far, most stay close to water. However, wood frogs often look for food in areas far from water.

The common frog can jump about 3 feet (91.4 centimeters). A bullfrog can leap nine times its body length. That's a jump of about 3.5 feet (1.1 meters). The southern cricket frog is only 1 inch (2.5 cm) long, but it can leap up to 8 feet (2.4 m)!

The Frog Life Cycle

A wood frog goes through many changes during its life. It starts out as a tiny egg. Then a tadpole hatches from this egg. A tadpole becomes a small froglet, which grows into an adult frog. Adult female frogs lay eggs, and the life cycle begins again.

Eggs

Adult Frog

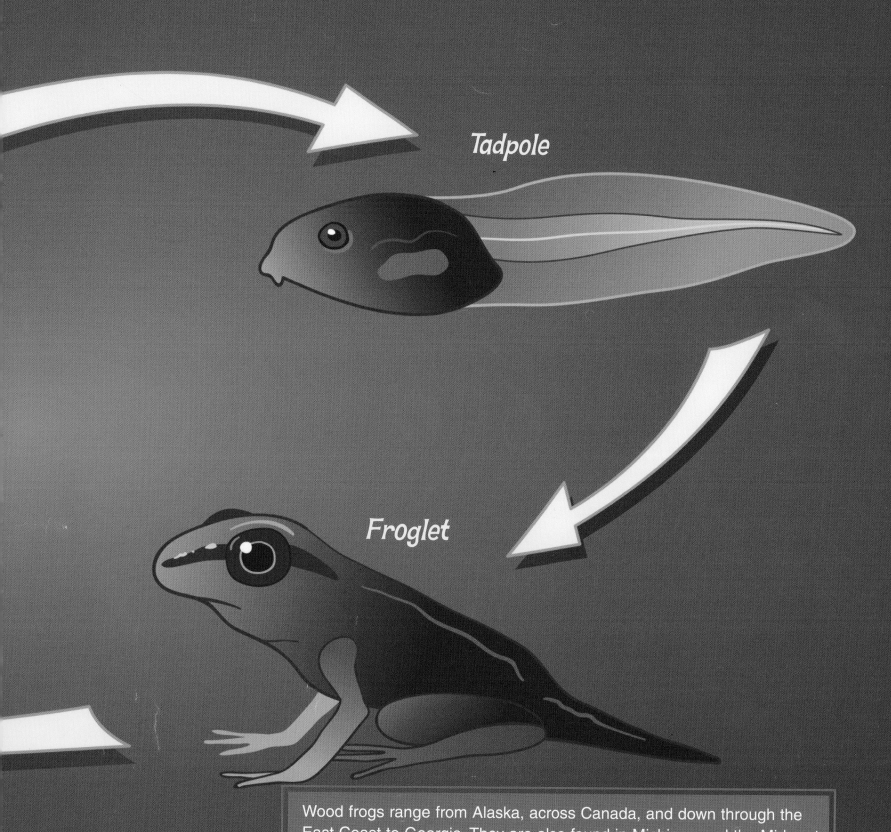

Tadpole

Froglet

Wood frogs range from Alaska, across Canada, and down through the East Coast to Georgia. They are also found in Michigan and the Midwest. They live farther north than any other North American frog.

A Mass of Eggs

In early spring, a female wood frog looks for a quiet pond in which to lay her eggs. She lays between 300 and 1,500 eggs at one time. She lays them beside those laid by other female wood frogs. Together, all of these eggs form a huge cluster, or group. A cluster often contains more than 150,000 eggs!

Each kind of female frog lays a different number of eggs. For example, a western chorus frog lays between 20 and 100 eggs, while the bullfrog lays 1,000 to 5,000 eggs.

Protecting the Tadpoles

In the center of a wood frog egg, a tiny tadpole starts to grow. A thick, clear jelly surrounds the growing tadpole. The jelly holds many frog eggs together. It also helps keep the eggs warm.

It's easy for scientists to study developing tadpoles. They can see through the jelly that surrounds each egg. Knowing how tadpoles grow helps scientists learn how other animals grow and change, too.

Tadpole

After about two weeks, a dark brown tadpole hatches from the egg. The tadpole swims around the pond by moving its long tail from side to side. It breathes through gills on the sides of its head. The gills are hidden behind a thin layer of skin. The tadpole eats a lot of food and grows quickly.

Most tadpoles eat small living things called algae. Tadpoles use their rows of tiny teeth to scrape algae off of objects on the bottom of a pond.

Metamorphosis

A tadpole's body goes through many changes. First, a tadpole grows back legs. Next, a tadpole grows lungs and loses its gills. Lungs allow a tadpole to breathe oxygen from the air. Finally, front legs begin to appear. These changes are called metamorphosis.

1. Tadpole

2. Tadpole with back legs

3. Tadpole with all four legs

Near the end of the tadpole stage, all four legs have finally grown. The back legs have five toes. The front legs have only four.

Land Living

Once a tadpole has all four legs, its tail begins to shrink. The tadpole leaves the water to become a froglet. A froglet tries out its new legs on land as it searches for insects to eat. The wood froglet spends most of its time in the woods, but it will also return to water. Once the froglet's tail disappears, metamorphosis is complete.

A wood frog eats insects such as beetles and flies. The frog's tongue is folded in half inside its mouth. When the frog is hungry, it quickly flips out its tongue to catch a flying snack.

A wood frog becomes an adult when it is about 2 years old. Early in spring, wood frogs hop to a nearby pond to mate. Male frogs croak loudly to attract the females. After mating, females lay eggs in the pond, and new frog life cycles begin.

Frogs do not mate at exactly the same time each year.
They must wait for the right air and water temperature.
Wood frogs usually mate in March or April.

Life Cycle of a Wood Frog

1. Egg
8–30 days

2. Tadpole
40–90 days

3. Froglet
1–2 years

4. Adult Frog
up to 6 years

Fun Facts

- The wood frog is known for its black "mask" and the fold that runs down its back. The animal is also known for its early mating. Wood frogs often move to mating sites while there is still snow on the ground and sometimes ice on the pond.

- The length of time a frog life cycle lasts depends on water temperature. For example, wood frog eggs laid in colder water can take one month to hatch. Eggs laid in warmer water may hatch in as little as eight days. Colder water also slows down growth in the tadpole and froglet stages.

Adult wood frog

- Frogs do not need to drink water because they take it in through their skin.

- Most frogs go into a deep sleep called torpor, or hibernation, during winter. As they sleep, frogs use the extra food they have stored in their bodies.

- The world is full of unusual frogs. The Goliath frog weighs up to 7 pounds (3.2 kilograms). This huge hopper lives in Africa. Wallace's flying frog is a small green frog that can use its black webbed feet as wings. It glides through the air from tree to tree.

- Frogs regularly shed their skin. Some shed their outer layer every few days. Other frogs will not shed for weeks. Most frogs eat this old skin.

Glossary

algae—plant-like living things in water that do not have roots or stems

amphibians—animals that live in water and on land

gill—a body part used to breathe underwater

mate—to join together to produce young

oxygen—a gas that people and animals must breathe to stay alive

predator—an animal that hunts and eats other animals

webbed—having skin that stretches between the toes

To Learn More

More Books to Read

Kalman, Bobbie, and Kathryn Smithyman. *The Life Cycle of a Frog.* New York: Crabtree Pub. Co., 2002.

Schwartz, David M. *Wood Frog.* Milwaukee: G. Stevens, 2001.

Zemlicka, Shannon. *From Tadpole to Frog.* Minneapolis: Lerner Publications Co., 2003.

Zoehfeld, Kathleen Weidner. *From Tadpole to Frog.* New York: Scholastic, 2002.

On the Web

FactHound offers a safe, fun way to find Web sites related to topics in this book. All of the sites on FactHound have been researched by our staff.

1. Visit *www.facthound.com*
2. Type in this special code: 140484922X
3. Click on the FETCH IT button.

Your trusty FactHound will fetch the best sites for you!

Index

Look for all of the books in the Amazing Science: Life Cycles series:

From Caterpillar to Butterfly: Following the Life Cycle
From Mealworm to Beetle: Following the Life Cycle
From Puppy to Dog: Following the Life Cycle
From Seed to Daisy: Following the Life Cycle
From Seed to Maple Tree: Following the Life Cycle
From Tadpole to Frog: Following the Life Cycle